THE REASON FOR CHRISTMAS

By

DAN HALFMAN

Dan Halfman
2021

ISBN 978-1-0980-5944-6 (hardcover)
ISBN 978-1-0980-5945-3 (digital)

Christian Faith Publishing, Inc.
832 Park Avenue
Meadville, PA 16335
www.christianfaithpublishing.com

Printed in the United States of America

for the gospel

for my children: reading to you has

always been and will always be one

of the best parts of my day

It's getting dark faster, the weather is colder.

Halloween candy is gone,

Thanksgiving is over.

This has happened before, this time of year,

when everything changes,

even the music I hear.

Away in a Manger, We Three Kings,

Hark! The Herald Angels Sing.

Up on the Housetop, Deck the Halls,

Jingle Bells, reindeer, I love them all!

Christmas Playlist

1. Away in a Manger

2. We Three Kings

3. Hark! The Herald Angels Sing

4. Up on the Housetop

5. Deck the Halls

6. Jingle Bells

7. Joy to the World

8. O Come All Ye Faithful

9. The First Noel

10. We Wish You a Merry Christmas

11. O Holy Night

12. God Rest Ye Merry Gentlemen

The house looks different, the things that I see.

There's lights and stockings and even a tree!

And on top of the tree there's a beautiful star.

At night I see lights when we drive in the car.

On the shelf I see toys I'm

not allowed to touch.

Mommy says no, even though

I want to so much!

She says they're important,

they're breakable, VERY!

The manger—Jesus, Joseph, and Mary!

I've seen Santa before, just

not up in the skies.

But I've never seen Jesus, at

least not with my eyes.

I sat on his lap, but it was at the mall.

I talk to Jesus each night,

what to make of it all!

Sometimes it's confusing,

I have to take pause.

Is Christmas for Christ or for Santa Claus?

I see Santa all over, he seems to have fame.

But Christmas, well, *CHRIST* is

right there in the name!

CHRISTMAS

I decide to investigate, look into the facts,

Examine it closely, expose any cracks.

I go up to my parents, they know a lot.

I ask them directly, put them on the spot.

"What's *the reason for Christmas*?

What's it all for?

Is it just about presents or

something much more?"

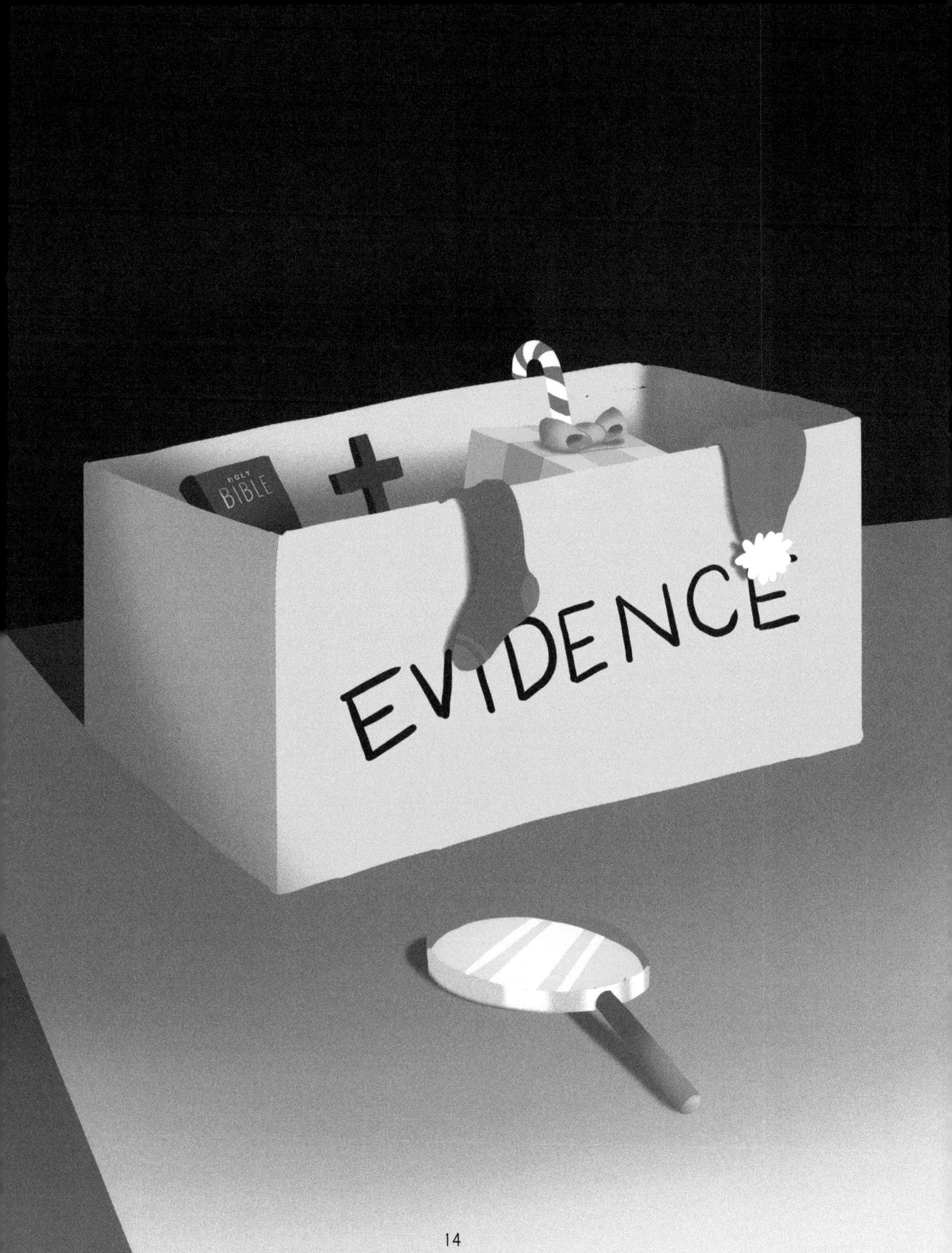
HOLY
BIBLE
EVIDENCE

They ask me to sit and tell me,

"That's a great question."

Then they take out a book and

say they have a suggestion.

They say, "This is the truth,

no use looking around."

The Bible is where they say

answers are found.

We start turning pages and

they ask me to hear

a story we've read before,

at least every year.

But this time it was different,

this time I was thinking.

I was thinking the words they

were reading were sinking.

By sinking I don't mean like

a boat going under,

but deeper into my heart, and

I started to wonder.

Luke 2:8-14 ESV

And in the same region there were shepherds out in the field, keeping watch over their flock by night. And an angel of the Lord appeared to them, and the glory of the Lord shone around them, and they were filled with great fear. And the angel said to them, "Fear not, for behold, I bring you good news of great joy that will be for all the people.

For unto you is born this day in the city of David a Savior, who is Christ the Lord. And this will be a sign for you: you will find a baby wrapped in swaddling cloths and lying in a manger." And suddenly there was with the angel a multitude of the heavenly host praising God and saying, "Glory to God in the highest, and on earth peace among those with whom he is pleased!"

So I asked, "What was the reason

for this story, this birth?

Why did Jesus leave heaven

and come down to earth?"

Again they turned to the Bible

and read together as one,

"For God so loved the world,

that he gave his only Son."

They went on to explain that

we are all sinners.

That we all miss the target, on

our own we're not winners.

But there's still GOOD NEWS, it's not a sad story.

If you believe in Jesus, you'll

be with him in glory!

What I came to decide

at the end of the day,

is believing in Santa is really okay.

But what's most important,

what I believe in my heart

is *the reason for Christmas* was only the start.

Jesus was born on Christmas, it's true.

And the reason he came was

to save me and you!

ABOUT THE AUTHOR

Dan Halfman is a Christian, a husband, and a father. He writes children's books that share the Gospel in a way that both children and adults can relate to. After reading many classic children's books to his own kids, Dan was inspired to use this method to deliver biblical truths to young readers. Lord willing, his books will help more people come to accept Jesus Christ as their Savior. Dan is a physical therapist in Ankeny, Iowa, where he lives with his amazing wife and wonderful children.

CPSIA information can be obtained
at www.ICGtesting.com
Printed in the USA
BVHW021522230321
603273BV00012B/730

9 781098 059446